MW00451537

Fishing

To

....

From

....

Date

....

Reflections at
First Light

Al Lindner & Ron Lindner

HARVEST HOUSE PUBLISHERS
EUGENE, OREGON

Reflections at First Light
Gift Book

Text copyright © 2015 by Al Lindner and Ron Lindner

Photography copyright © 2015 by Bill Lindner Photography

Published by Harvest House Publishers • Eugene, Oregon 97402 • www.harvesthousepublishers.com

ISBN 978-0-7369-6427-2

Design and production by Left Coast Design, Portland, Oregon

Harvest House Publishers has made every effort to trace the ownership of all poems and quotes.
In the event of a question arising from the use of a poem or quote, we regret any error made
and will be pleased to make the necessary correction in future editions of this book.

Unless otherwise indicated, all Scripture quotations are taken from the Holy Bible, New International Version®,
NIV®. Copyright © 1973, 1978, 1984, 2011 by Biblica, Inc.® Used by permission. All rights reserved worldwide.

Verses marked NKJV are taken from the New King James Version®. Copyright © 1982 by Thomas Nelson, Inc.
Used by permission. All rights reserved.

ALL RIGHTS RESERVED. No part of this publication may be reproduced, stored in a retrieval system,
or transmitted in any form or by any means—electronic, mechanical, digital, photocopy, recording, or any
other—except for brief quotations in printed reviews, without the prior permission of the publisher.

PRINTED IN CHINA

15 16 17 18 19 20 21 22 / DS / 10 9 8 7 6 5 4 3 2 1

To our Lord and Savior Jesus Christ, and to His laborers who shared the saving gospel with us—Evangelist Lowell Lundstrom and Pastor David Sorenson.

To our wives, Dolores and Mary, who not only raised our families during our early years of being on the road for long periods of time, but also remained steadfast partners as we built our businesses together.

And to the many folks we have worked with and learned from, whose names indeed would cover this entire page.

I can't remember a time when I didn't fish. My earliest recollections are of summers I stayed with my grandmother on a lake near Hayward, Wisconsin. I spent countless hours fishing from the shore, wading, and occasionally fishing with my uncles in a boat. I also fished with my brother Ron, who is ten years my senior. If I dug the worms, seined the minnows, fixed the tackle, and loaded the boat, he would take me out with him. He told me everyone starts out as a "worm boy" apprentice, and for years I believed him. —Al

Fishing

.030 x 2½ SHAFT

⅛ HOLLOW
METAL BEADS (2)

COIL SPRING FASTE
.064 ¼ LONG

EASY SPIN
CLEVIS

#3 BRASS
CRIMPED LOCKS

#6 TRE
3553

PAINTED HEAD

LARGE RIPPLED ¹#
BLADE — GOLD
NICKEL OR TIGER FINISH

LINDNER MF
SPIN MINN

From 1967 to 1979, I sometimes logged as many as 300 days on the water in a single year. All this time, the God I didn't know or care about not only allowed me to have these experiences but also kept me safe. God had a plan for my life that would turn my all-consuming passion for fishing into a lifestyle that was both acceptable and useful to Him. Not surprisingly, a few changes were in order—changes that dramatically impacted my "fish all the time" obsession.

When I received Jesus as Lord of my life, I was relieved that He did not ask me to go into some other endeavor. I was in my late thirties, and fishing was the only thing I knew how to do. He graciously allowed me to continue to fish hard in the coming decades, but He made certain that the intensity of my earlier years gave way to a more balanced mode of living. —*Al*

There is always a little boy
in the old man gone fishing.
anonymous

When I started attending church regularly, my eyes were opened, and I devoured the Bible as I once did books on fishing. I was thrilled to learn that many of Jesus's first inductees (the apostles) were fishermen and that Jesus was evidently well acquainted with life in the boat.

As I started to share my Christian faith with others, most of whom were fellow fishermen, I found myself naturally using fishing experiences to illustrate and explain the workings of the kingdom of God. I sensed that God, the supreme conservationist, did not intend to waste all of my earlier efforts and experiences. Instead, God used for His own purposes the gift He had given me for fishing and the experiences Ron and I accumulated through our many years as professional anglers. —*Al*

My brother Ron, his wife, Dolores, and my wife, Mary, had all dedicated their lives to the Lord, and I was the single holdout. Our kids were attending a private Christian school, and I often attended functions where the gospel message was proclaimed loud and clear. God was priming me. Members of my television audience began sending me fan mail and including gospel tracts. I started reconnecting with old carousing buddies whose lives had been completely transformed. Amazing changes were happening all around me. Clearly, somebody was trying to get my attention.

At age 37, I finally surrendered. I came to faith in Jesus Christ and said a simple prayer, confessing with my mouth that Jesus is Lord and believing in my heart that God raised Him from the dead (Romans 10:9-10). I was born again right there in my living room. Just as I finished my prayer, our grandfather clock chimed. That defining moment determined my destiny and changed the direction of my life—forever! —Al

We may say of angling as Dr. Boteler
said of strawberries: 'Doubtless God could
have made a better berry, but doubtless
God never did,' and so, if I may be judge,
God never did make a more calm, quiet,
innocent recreation than angling.
Sir Izaak Walton

Good things come to those who bait.

anonymous

Looking back, I can clearly see God's leading hand in my life. Al calls them "God nudges." They are incidents in our lives that we fully understand only when looking back through the prism of time. We all have them in one form or another. They are direct interventions that can come only from God and that turn our sails and chart a new course for our lives. Thinking back, all of us could probably write books chronicling the many twists and turns we've experienced—wins, losses, detours, and out-of-the-blue urgings from God. —*Ron*

Even a bad day of
fishing is better than
a good day of work.
anonymous

Of all the things we have printed or aired on television over the years, the one that has prompted the most heart-searching questions, comments, and opinions was our fish symbol. For us it has a long and hallowed history.

In the early '80s, the Christian fish symbol was not displayed nearly as widely as it is today. An occasional bumper sticker was about all you were likely to see. Dolores had put a fish symbol on their mailbox at home. Ron decided to put one on his boat as well. That was it, and no one thought much more about it.

But Ron began dabbling with it more and more, adding a cross to the fish and trying some variations in conjunction with our logo. Ron, Dolores, Mary, and I had already agreed that we would put the words, "Jesus Is Lord" over the entry of our building. When the sign was mounted, we held hands and prayed, dedicating our company to God. With that dedication, we also decided to add the fish symbol to our corporate logo. The public display of the fish symbol reminds us that we are to depend on God as our source and not look to any other place or to anyone else. —*Al*

I am constantly amazed by the many ways God meets us and how often He communicates through what we are familiar with. God has often used lures, rods, and boats to teach us fishing-related lessons we can easily identify with. The psalmist David had been a shepherd, and he understood God's goodness in terms of green pastures and still waters. The apostle Peter, an experienced fisherman, knew that God supplies all our needs and can even put a coin in a fish's mouth to help him out.

Because God loves us, He wants us to be familiar with His Word (the Scriptures). If we listen closely, we can hear Him speaking to us in His still, small voice deep inside. —*Al*

Smooth runs the water
where the brook is deep.
William Shakespeare

Not so long ago we had the opportunity to engage in a legal battle, but in prayer, we received assurance that we were not to open that door. Individually, we were led to Jesus's words "Shake the dust off your feet" (Luke 9:5). Yes, the Scriptures provide the wisdom we need to avoid fleshly entanglements. We've never been to court since. —*Al*

In all things of nature there is something of the marvelous.
Aristotle

The charm
of fishing is that
it is the pursuit of
what is elusive
but attainable,
a perpetual series
of occasions
for hope.
John Buchan

As a competitor who loves to win, I was totally disheartened after performing poorly at a big tournament. But as I drove home across the country, I realized that I am amazingly blessed. I live in this great nation of ours. I am free to pursue my dreams and make a fine living doing what I love—fishing! I support myself through a lifestyle, not a job. And I had just fished with some of the best fishermen in the world on legendary waters with beautiful facilities and every convenience.

Can anyone who gets to do what I do ever complain that they had a bad day fishing?

One of the primary reasons God was not pleased with the children of Israel during their exodus was their murmuring and complaining. A good reminder. —Al

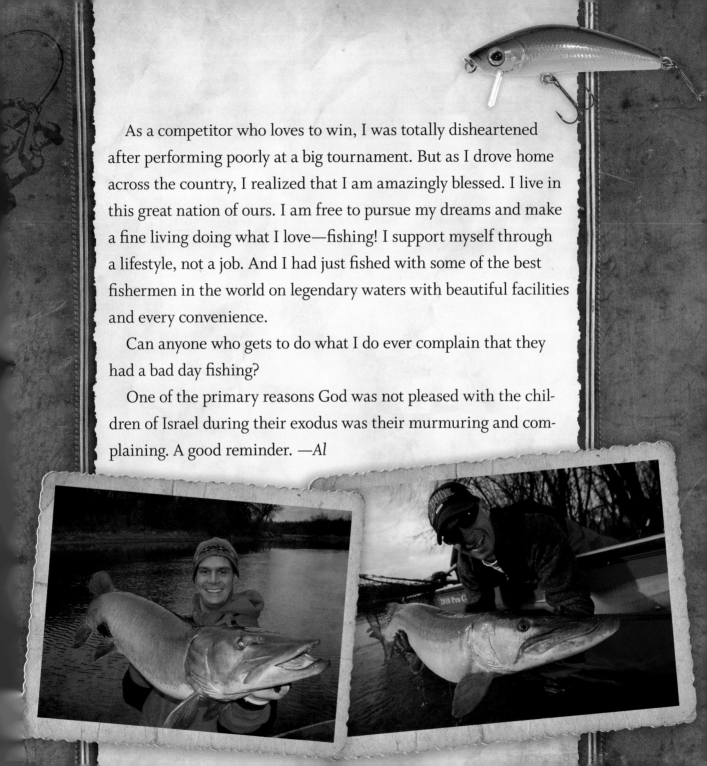

The peace of God that eventually came over Al after that discouraging tournament was like the calm and serenity of a quiet river as the wind dies down. Contentment is not a life free from trouble or challenges. But when the peace of God comes to rule in our hearts, and when the joy of the Lord becomes our strength, the sense of divine blessing overflows in us! Then we can say with David, "Why, my soul, are you downcast? Why so disturbed within me? Put your hope in God, for I will yet praise him, my Savior and my God" (Psalm 42:5).

—*Mary Linder*

There is certainly something in angling that
tends to produce a serenity of the mind.
Washington Irving

Something is magical about the twilight hours on a northern lake in late fall. The flickering sunshine reflects off the ice all around and falls softly into the hushed seclusion of the lake. I love the long, slanting bars of light that strike the treetops around the edge of the water and the deep shadows on the hills. The trees, though stripped and bare except for a few brown leaves, stand tall and strong to face the cool, bracing air of early winter. —*Al*

The ice suddenly cracked without warning. I fell
through, plunging forward into the freezing
water. My right arm caught at the elbow
on the other end of the ice, and instantly
my full weight jerked my right shoulder back
really hard. The back of my shoulder pushed
all the way out—I thought I'd just dislocated
my shoulder—and then…everything…went
blank.

I remember nothing of what happened
next. Nothing. The lights went out, outer
silence became inner silence,
and I sensed nothing.
The next thing I remember is kneeling on the
ice at the edge of the hole, soaking wet. I took a
deep breath and gazed around, searching the ice
for the person who pulled me out of the water.
No one was on the ice but me, yet I knew I
couldn't have possibly pulled myself out.

Perhaps you believe there's a natural expla-
nation for how I made it home that night, but
I can tell you that if an angel hadn't been walk-
ing beside me on the lake, I would have been a goner.

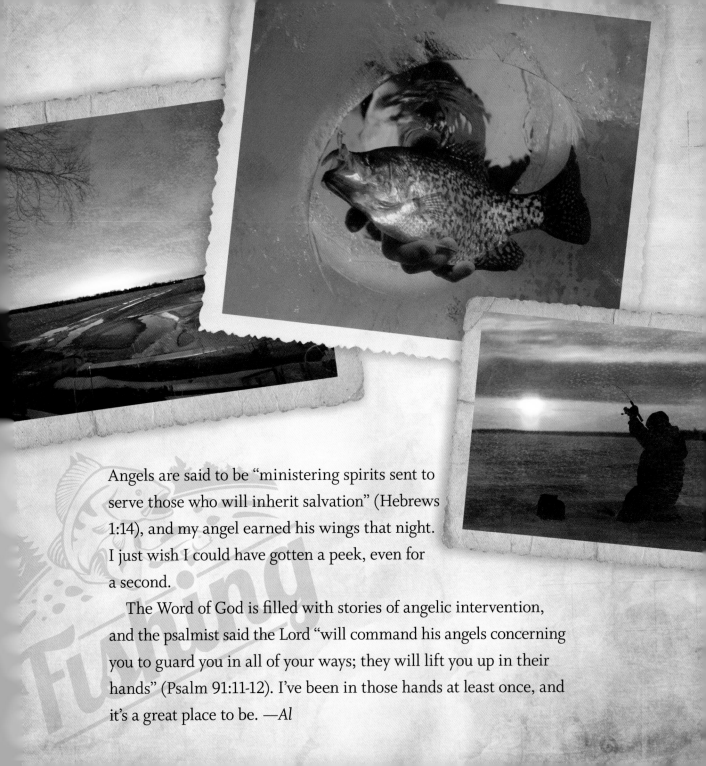

Angels are said to be "ministering spirits sent to serve those who will inherit salvation" (Hebrews 1:14), and my angel earned his wings that night. I just wish I could have gotten a peek, even for a second.

The Word of God is filled with stories of angelic intervention, and the psalmist said the Lord "will command his angels concerning you to guard you in all of your ways; they will lift you up in their hands" (Psalm 91:11-12). I've been in those hands at least once, and it's a great place to be. —*Al*

In 1984, after considerable prayer and godly counsel, we felt certain of God's blessing to purchase a summer camp for kids. It was situated on three small, beautifully wooded lakes just south of Leech Lake near Walker, Minnesota. Kids' activities dominated the summer, and after Labor Day we also ran an outreach at the camp that became known as the Fishers of Men Retreats.

At our first retreat, fishermen who were born again each invited a fisherman who was searching for the truth. Each Christian was asked to pray for his guest for the entire week preceding this retreat. Everyone attended a morning session by our evangelist, and then searchers were paired with believers to go out in the boats—but not with the person who brought them. The focus was to allow the Holy Spirit to work and speak through our lives while enjoying days of great fishing.

After dinner there was another hour or so of explaining the simple gospel, focusing only on God's biblical plan for salvation. Then we broke into small groups, and questions were encouraged. Many hours of good discussions took place in the solitude around a bonfire and under a beautiful starlit sky.

The last session before everyone returned home, the evangelist asked those who wanted to turn their life and will over to Jesus to stand up. On that first retreat, everyone did, and many made verbal confessions for Jesus. For the attendees as well as for Al and me and our Christian friends who had come along to speak and give counsel, it lived up to its billing as the "fishing trip of a lifetime"—both for fish and for men. —*Ron*

The Bible states that "neither the one who plants nor the one who waters is anything, but only God, who makes things grow" (1 Corinthians 3:7), and we saw this demonstrated over and over at the camp. We watched as individuals whose loved ones had prayed for them for years finally surrendered to Jesus Christ. Others who had walked away from faith in Christ for a time returned to Him at our retreats. Some left the camp without making a decision but later contacted us to say thanks for their special weekend and to tell us they had since become Christians. We never did an actual follow-up, but we know that a high percentage of the men came to faith. And many believers said the weekends strengthened their walk with Christ and motivated them to make positive changes in their lives. —*Ron*

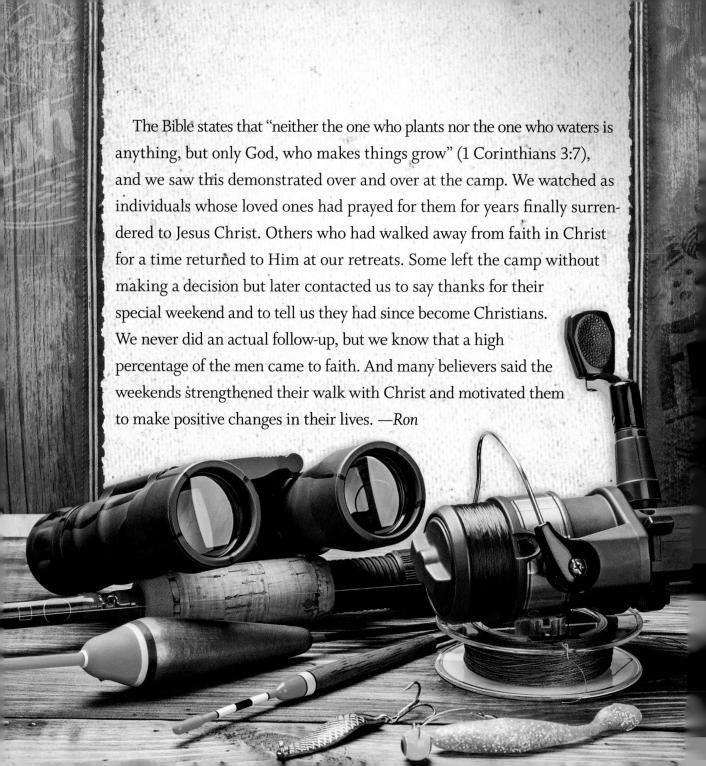

All I have seen teaches me to trust
the creator for all I have not seen.
Ralph Waldo Emerson

Today, God continues to work through men who came to Christ at the camp. One is building churches in Russia. Another is a senior member of a large national Christian youth ministry. An optometrist who accepted Jesus replicated the retreats in Wisconsin. A chiropractor is doing the same in Ontario, Canada.

We know that many men were reconciled with their families and are active Christians today, bringing other family members and friends into the kingdom of God. And as an extra-special gift from the Lord to me, one of my sons came to accept Jesus at one of those retreats.

After we sold the camp, we continued to conduct periodic Fishers of Men Retreats in different locales. And in conjunction with large tackle firms, the extensive fishing curriculum and materials we developed for teaching were donated to the US Fish and Wildlife Service and used at sites across the country to instruct kids. Parts of these are still in use today. —*Ron*

Everybody needs beauty as well as bread, places to play in and pray in, where nature may heal and give strength to body and soul alike.

John Muir

One morning while running on the treadmill, I began to ask, "What do you have next for me, Lord?"

I clearly sensed a response in my heart. "I want you to get back into television, but this time I want you to reference My Word and the things I have done in your life."

I could see it—a brief spiritual and inspirational closing of some kind at the end of every fishing show, planting seeds in the hearts of those who love to fish but would never tune in to a religious program.

Including a spiritual message in our show on secular television stations and networks was a huge endeavor, and we had no idea how it would be received. In 2003 the spiritual climate was not what it is in 2015. A lot has changed in the past decade or so—and not always for the better. Yet I am happy to report that the response of the viewing public to the ending of our show has been overwhelmingly positive through the years. As a testimony to God's faithfulness, in 2015 we are celebrating our forty-fifth consecutive year on television. Thank You, Lord Jesus. —*Al*

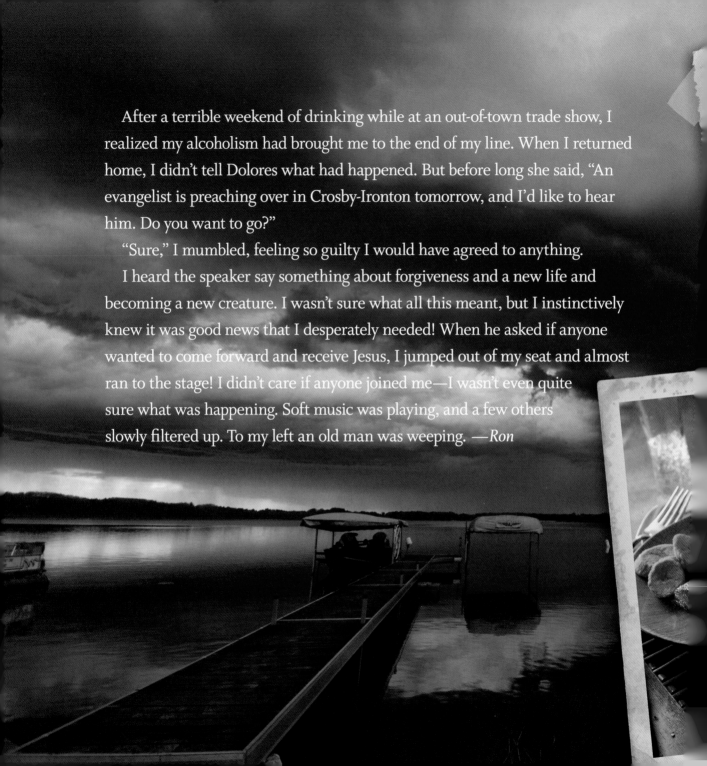

After a terrible weekend of drinking while at an out-of-town trade show, I realized my alcoholism had brought me to the end of my line. When I returned home, I didn't tell Dolores what had happened. But before long she said, "An evangelist is preaching over in Crosby-Ironton tomorrow, and I'd like to hear him. Do you want to go?"

"Sure," I mumbled, feeling so guilty I would have agreed to anything.

I heard the speaker say something about forgiveness and a new life and becoming a new creature. I wasn't sure what all this meant, but I instinctively knew it was good news that I desperately needed! When he asked if anyone wanted to come forward and receive Jesus, I jumped out of my seat and almost ran to the stage! I didn't care if anyone joined me—I wasn't even quite sure what was happening. Soft music was playing, and a few others slowly filtered up. To my left an old man was weeping. —*Ron*

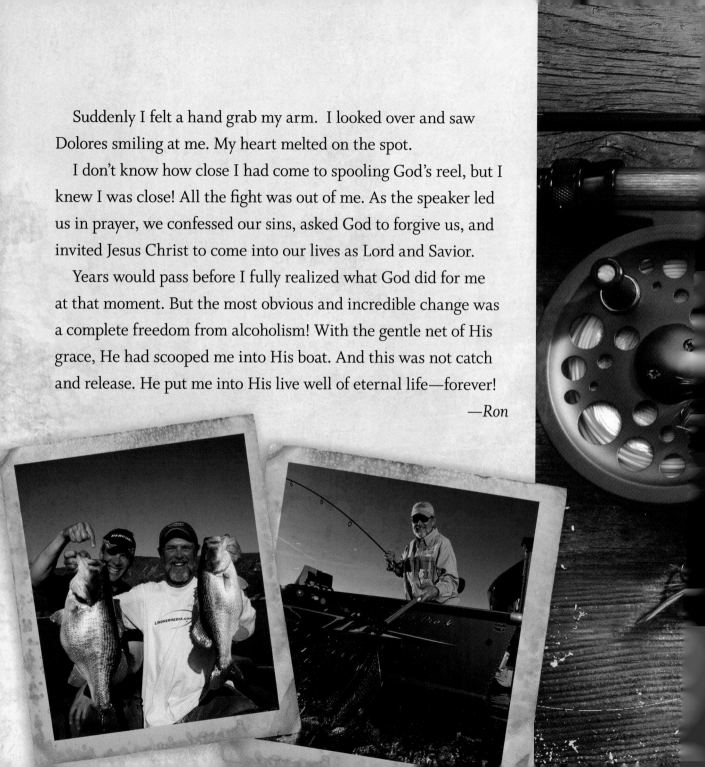

Suddenly I felt a hand grab my arm. I looked over and saw Dolores smiling at me. My heart melted on the spot.

I don't know how close I had come to spooling God's reel, but I knew I was close! All the fight was out of me. As the speaker led us in prayer, we confessed our sins, asked God to forgive us, and invited Jesus Christ to come into our lives as Lord and Savior.

Years would pass before I fully realized what God did for me at that moment. But the most obvious and incredible change was a complete freedom from alcoholism! With the gentle net of His grace, He had scooped me into His boat. And this was not catch and release. He put me into His live well of eternal life—forever!

—*Ron*

Looking back on my life, the biggest snag to my finding true happiness was my complete misunderstanding of God's love and grace. Only after years of abusive drinking and a blackout weekend did I begin to understand that salvation is a free gift of God that comes to us by faith. We can never earn or merit it. We simply need to believe the truth that Jesus Christ gave His life and blood to forgive us of our sins. It's that easy!

Perhaps you have run out of tomorrows and dragged yourself out to the end of the line. If you want to find peace with God, remember, "If you declare with your mouth, 'Jesus is Lord,' and believe in your heart that God raised him from the dead, you will be saved" (Romans 10:9). If you will receive Jesus Christ into your life today, He will come in and change you in ways you never imagined.

After receiving Jesus at the Crosby meeting, later that night I sat alone in our living room, reading and rereading a little booklet called *Saved for Sure*. Over and over in my mind I was pondering, *Is it really this simple?* As my eye glanced out the picture window overlooking the lake at two thirty in the morning, I saw the northern lights explode into the night sky like never before or since. A colossal celestial celebration welcomed me into God's kingdom. —*Ron*

The lakes are something which you are unprepared for; they lie up
so high, exposed to the light, and the forest is diminished to a fine fringe
on their edges, with here and there a blue mountain, like amethyst jewels set
around some jewel of the first water,—so anterior, so superior, to all the
changes that are to take place on their shores, even now
civil and refined, and fair as they can ever be.

Henry David Thoreau

Al and I have lived most of our lives doing what we love to do, and fishing has never grown old. When it's first light on the water, we want to be there, and at the end of the day, it's still hard to take that last cast. I'd like a nickel for every cast I've made after saying, "Just one more."

Before we close this book, however, we'd like to take one last cast in your direction. You've read our stories, and you've seen some of the ways our faith has influenced the decisions we've had to make along life's long road. It's possible that you're not certain what Al and I mean when we say we're born-again Christians. —*Ron*

When Jesus spoke the words "You must be born again" to Nicodemus in the third chapter of the Gospel of John, He did not simply offer a good idea, a nice suggestion, or something Nicodemus might consider as an option or alternative to something else. As a Pharisee, Nicodemus was already a deeply religious man. As a member of the Sanhedrin, the supreme council of the Jews, he was a national leader. Nicodemus certainly didn't need to become more religious—he was already stuffed to the gills with religion. Jesus said that to enter the kingdom of God, one must first have his or her heart changed. Nicodemus (and I) struggled to understand this.

I've heard many phrases used to describe the process of salvation —"making Jesus Lord of your life," "accepting Jesus as your personal Savior," "coming to the cross," "making a decision for Christ," "having a personal relationship with Jesus," "confessing Christ as Lord"…and the list goes on and on. Still, the process of being born again, regardless of what it's called, comes down to this: We acknowledge we are sinners, we repent (turn away from our sin), we accept through faith that only through Jesus's death, burial, and resurrection can we be forgiven and have our sins washed away, and we ask Jesus to come into our hearts through the Holy Spirit and make us new people. —*Ron*

"As no man is born an artist,
so no man is born an angler."
Sir Izaak Walton

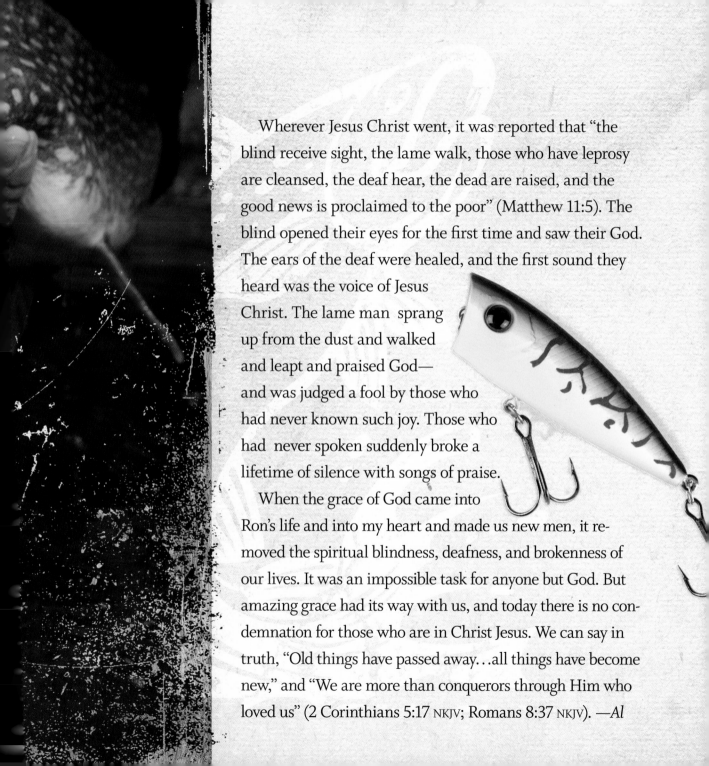

Wherever Jesus Christ went, it was reported that "the blind receive sight, the lame walk, those who have leprosy are cleansed, the deaf hear, the dead are raised, and the good news is proclaimed to the poor" (Matthew 11:5). The blind opened their eyes for the first time and saw their God. The ears of the deaf were healed, and the first sound they heard was the voice of Jesus Christ. The lame man sprang up from the dust and walked and leapt and praised God— and was judged a fool by those who had never known such joy. Those who had never spoken suddenly broke a lifetime of silence with songs of praise.

When the grace of God came into Ron's life and into my heart and made us new men, it removed the spiritual blindness, deafness, and brokenness of our lives. It was an impossible task for anyone but God. But amazing grace had its way with us, and today there is no condemnation for those who are in Christ Jesus. We can say in truth, "Old things have passed away...all things have become new," and "We are more than conquerors through Him who loved us" (2 Corinthians 5:17 NKJV; Romans 8:37 NKJV). —*Al*

Today there are many new philosophies, new revelations, and new ways of trying to please God (or gods). I see people chasing after them to try to seize this or that promise, only to return hungrier and thirstier than ever. Don't go that way. True faith in Jesus will deliver you from any emptiness. Grace will flow into your heart, and delivering mercy will be the anchor of your life.

When Christ is in your heart, real life is possible, joy is possible, and peace is possible—in all circumstances and all places. Everything your redeemed soul can desire, it possesses in Christ. Endless "rivers of life" flow in and through those who have Jesus in their hearts. —*Al*

A lake is the landscape's most beautiful and expressive feature. It is earth's eye; looking into which the beholder measures the depth of his own nature.

Henry David Thoreau